Faith in Action" Series

NO COMPROMISE

THE STORY OF DIETRICH BONHOEFFER

Audrey Constant

RELIGIOUS AND MORAL EDUCATION PRESS

Religious and Moral Education Press
An imprint of Chansitor Publications Ltd
A Subsidiary Company of Hymns Ancient & Modern Ltd
St Mary's Works, St Mary's Plain
Norwich, Norfolk NR3 3BH

Photographs are reproduced by courtesy of
Chr. Kaiser Verlag (pp. 2, 3, 5, 9, 20, 23) and BBC Hulton Picture
Library (p. 17)

First published 1983
Reprinted 1993

Printed in Great Britain by BPCC Wheatons Ltd, Hennock Road, Exeter

ISBN 1 85175 014 2

NO COMPROMISE

The Story of Dietrich Bonhoeffer

Some people of great faith have spent their lives working for others. The work of Doctor Barnardo and Mother Teresa, for example, has helped many thousands of people in need. But there are also people whose faith has helped others in a less direct way.

Dietrich Bonhoeffer (pronounced *Bon*hoffer) dedicated his life to preaching the gospel of Jesus Christ and living according to His teachings. When his faith brought him into conflict with Hitler's Nazis, he stood firm in his belief. His refusal to compromise made him feared and hated by those in authority and eventually cost him his life.

Dietrich Bonhoeffer helped (and still helps) other people because his life was an inspiring example to follow, a story of great courage and steadfast faith.

His early life

Dietrich and his twin sister, Sabine, were born on 4 February 1906 in Breslau (now called Wroclaw), Germany. Together with six other brothers and sisters, they were brought up in a happy, well-to-do home. Their father,

The Bonhoeffers in 1909, shortly after the birth of the youngest child, Susanne (Dietrich is second from right)

a professor, expected a great deal of his children. From an early age they were taught the importance of thinking and speaking clearly, and they were encouraged to stand up for what they thought was right.

Dietrich's parents didn't worry too much about torn clothes or broken windows; they put consideration of the needs and feelings of other people first. A concern for the weak, who could not speak up for themselves, remained with Dietrich all his life.

When Dietrich was about six years old, the Bonhoeffers moved to Berlin. The Professor took up a post as Director of Psychiatry in a large hospital there. The upper part of the Bonhoeffer's house was given over to the children. Here they played and had parties, often joined by their mother. Downstairs it was another matter. Their father was in charge there, and they had to be on their best behaviour.

Dietrich was a high-spirited boy, and on more than one occasion had his ears boxed by his mother for misbehaving.

The Bonhoeffers were not a church-going family, but their mother made sure the children knew the Bible and the hymns she herself loved. All family weddings, baptisms and funerals were performed in the house by an uncle who was a pastor.

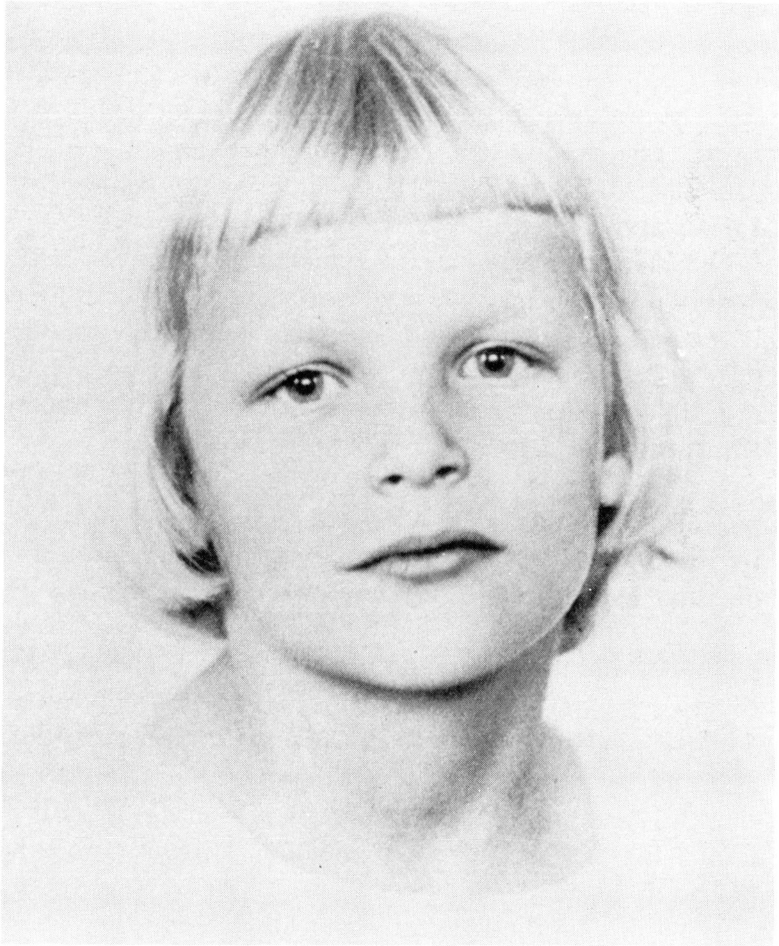

Dietrich aged seven

Dietrich was eight when the First World War broke out. As news of the war casualties came through, he and Sabine had long conversations about death and eternity and tried to imagine what it was like to be dead. When, in the spring of 1918, their eldest brother was killed at the front, Dietrich was overcome by grief. He became haunted by a fear of death. It was then that he began to think seriously about God.

Life was not all gloomy. There were times of hilarious fun and happiness. In the summer, the family used to go to the Harz Mountains and the children ran wild in the hills and forests. Dietrich sometimes left the others and spent hours reading in the meadows. He loved stories of courage and daring, and often read Bible stories.

One of his companions later remembered how, when they were about fourteen, they used to discuss religious subjects. It was always Dietrich who answered their questions, often replying with another question which led more deeply into the subject. Even at that time Dietrich could not tolerate empty talk or insincerity.

Dietrich had always been a very good musician and his parents thought he might train as a professional pianist. But by the time he was fourteen, he was already coming to a decision about his future. One day his teacher asked the students what they wanted to do when they left school. Dietrich announced quietly that he was going to study theology. "Now," he thought, "I've committed myself. There's no going back." His unexpected answer had drawn attention and admiration from the other pupils. The fact that this gave him pleasure seemed to him a form of vanity, a fault in his character he must overcome. This was something he had to battle with all his life.

When his brothers heard about his decision they teased him about it and tried to persuade him that such a life would never suit him. By now Dietrich was a strong, good-looking boy, good at games and outstandingly gifted at school. He was popular and fun to be with, and they thought he could make a career for himself in almost anything he chose. Why then should he choose a boring subject like theology? But Dietrich's mind was made up.

His training

At the age of seventeen Dietrich went to Tübingen University to begin his religious studies. His first year there seemed to make little impression on him, but the following spring he set out with his brother Klaus on a three-month

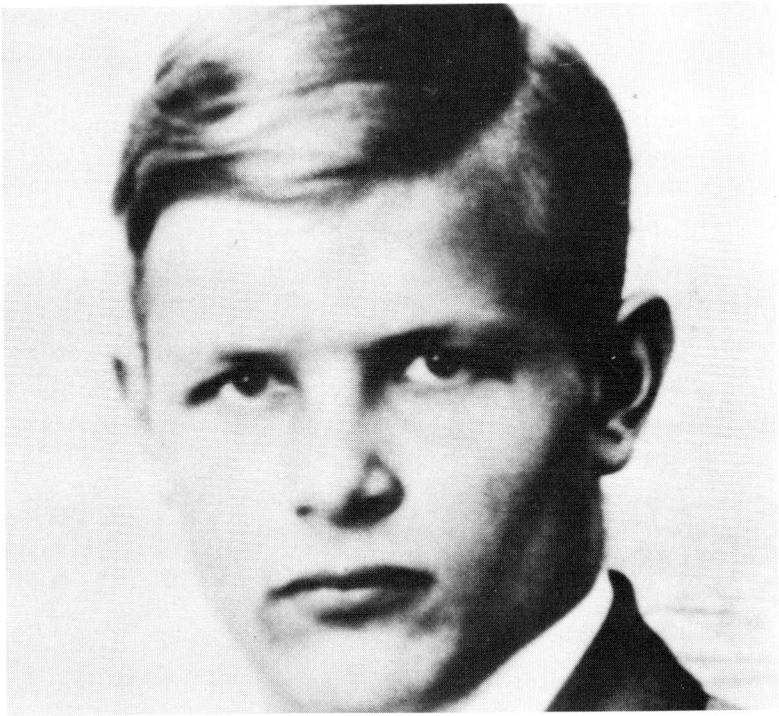

Dietrich in 1923

visit to Rome. Klaus was an artist; he was thrilled with the beauty of the city. Dietrich, on the other hand, found his attention drawn to the Roman Catholic Church. His first High Mass on Palm Sunday in St Peter's affected him deeply.

The following year (1924) Dietrich went to study at Berlin University. He worked hard and enrolled for many different lectures. He did not always agree with his professors and did not hesitate to argue his point.

Every theological student had to do some practical parish work for the first examination and Dietrich took over a children's service in a nearby church. He loved these young people and invited groups of them to his house and organised expeditions and games for them. The older ones were keen to learn a lot more than he could teach them at church, so he arranged discussions with them at home.

Although he was a dedicated student, Dietrich found time to enjoy himself. At week-ends he invited his friends to stay, gave parties and played the piano and danced with them. He was naturally good at sport and, while others had to practise hard to win, he could leave his books for an afternoon and win a high-jump competition with what seemed little effort.

When he was twenty-two he went to Barcelona to work and preached to a German Lutheran community there. The elderly pastor gave him a free hand and Dietrich threw himself into the life surrounding the church. Soon the congregation doubled. The parishioners found that this young man made the Christian faith come alive for them.

In the spring of 1929 Dietrich returned to his studies in Berlin and became a fully qualified preacher. But he had to wait another eighteen months, until he was twenty-five, before he could enter the Church. In the meantime he was invited to spend a year at the Union Theological Seminary in New York.

His first visit to America

In September 1930 Dietrich left for America. He found life there very different from the life he had known in his homeland. In Germany he had treated his professors with formal courtesy. American students treated theirs as equals and were on Christian-name terms with them. Most of the theological students were older than himself and, in his opinion, had not the faintest idea what theology was about. But, in his easy, charming way, Dietrich quickly made many friends.

He felt that Americans took neither life nor their studies as seriously as did his fellow students in Germany, and that their conversation was without depth. He felt more in sympathy with a black student, Frank Fisher, who found in Dietrich an understanding listener. At that time black people were looked down on in America and most of them lived in poverty.

One day Dietrich took Frank to an expensive restaurant. When he was told that his friend could not be served because he was black, Dietrich walked out, furious.

As their friendship deepened, Frank confided in Dietrich about his people's sufferings and took him to his home in Harlem. It was not long before Dietrich was taking an active part in the Christian life of the community. He was impressed by the deep faith of these black people and by the joy of their worship. Every Sunday he went to a large Baptist church in Harlem and led a group of young people in Sunday School. He also led a women's Bible-study class.

Return to Germany

At the end of the year Dietrich returned to a Germany crushed by economic depression. It was late 1931, when seven million people in Germany were unemployed and millions were starving. In all this suffering, the Church seemed to be giving no help or guidance. "What is the use of all our theology in times like these?" Dietrich asked himself. He felt powerless to do anything to help his countrymen.

In 1931 he became a fully fledged pastor. It had struck him that pastors often preached on social problems rather than on the gospel of Jesus Christ. When he stood up to preach a sermon, he spoke simply but did not make Christianity sound easy. Instead he stressed how much people owed Jesus Christ, who had died for their sins, and reminded the congregation of their duty as Christians. This did not frighten them away. In fact, more and more people came to listen to him, people who grew to love and respect him.

On 1 August 1931 he was appointed lecturer at the University of Berlin, but he found the work dull. Many of his ideas differed from those of the other professors and some grew suspicious of him. Just as Dietrich was becoming restless and disheartened, he was asked to take over a confirmation class of fifty unruly boys in one of the toughest districts of working-class Berlin.

An elderly pastor took him to meet the boys. As they climbed the stairs of the school building, boys hung over the bannisters throwing rubbish down on their heads. At the top, the old pastor tried to push the boys into the class-room and shouted that he had brought a new pastor to teach them. They laughed when they heard his name was Bonhoeffer and started chanting, "Bon, bon, bon!" The old man left, abandoning Dietrich to his fate.

He leaned against the wall with his hands in his pockets, watching the boys. Gradually the shouting died down. Dietrich began to speak, very quietly. Only the boys close to him could hear and the others wanted to listen too. Suddenly the whole class stood silent. Dietrich just said that they had put up a remarkable performance for him. Then he told them a short story about Harlem. They wanted to hear more, but Dietrich dismissed them and said there would be more next time. He had won their attention.

From then on he devoted more and more time to the boys, and early in the following year he rented a room near the school. He told his landlady that the boys were to be allowed in his room even when he wasn't there. They had never been trusted like this before and they appreciated it.

Every evening the boys came to Dietrich's room and there was always something there for them to eat. Before they left he used to read out a passage from the Bible for them to discuss.

None of the boys had decent clothes, so, as their confirmation day drew near, he bought a bale of cloth and cut it up to make suits for them. As they watched, he asked them what they hoped to hear in his confirmation sermon. They answered, "We would like a serious warning which we shall remember all our lives."

Dietrich with some of his confirmation students

But when Dietrich stood up to preach at the boys' confirmation, he told them that he could not make the future seem harder and darker than it already was. "Today you are not to be given fear of life, but courage," he said. "So I want to give you the hope that we have and which no one can take from you. If God be for us, who can be against us?"

A few days later he took the boys to stay with him at his parents' house, although he had to leave early to attend a Youth Commission conference, as the representative of Berlin University.

It was at this conference that Dietrich first met Bishop Bell of Chichester, a man who was later to play a leading role in the struggle of the German Church against Hitler.

Hitler's rise to power

On 30 January 1933 Adolf Hitler came to power. Many German people, hoping that a change of government would solve their problems, voted for Hitler's National Socialist Party (known as the Nazi Party). The Nazis swept in with a large majority at the general election and Hitler became the Chancellor, or Prime Minister.

Conditions in Germany had become so bad that the people were willing to work hard and sacrifice their own wishes in order to make the country great again. So when Hitler's firm government seemed to be bringing the problem of unemployment under control, and improving life for many people, a wave of hope and enthusiasm swept the country. However, it was soon clear to some (including Dietrich) that the improvements were being made at the cost of personal freedom.

Four weeks after Hitler became Chancellor, the Reichstag (pronounced Rike-stahg), the German parliament building, burnt to the ground. Although no one ever discovered

On 6/11/32. The last democratic election for many years was held. The Nazis lost 2 million votes and 34 seats reducing its deputies to (196). The Communists had (100) seats. Socialist party had (121). National party had (52). A sinister camarilla in which Franz von Papen, Kurt Schleicher and Hindenburg were the prime intriguers, manoeuvred Hitler and the Nazis into power on 30/1/33.

exactly how this happened, Hitler used the incident to tighten his hold over the nation.

New laws were passed which were supposed to be "for the protection of the nation", but which in fact increased Hitler's power. The laws limited personal freedom, freedom of speech and the freedom of the press. Public gatherings and the formation of societies were forbidden. The government now had the right to search houses and take over private property. Telephones were tapped and letters opened. Anyone who disobeyed the laws was severely punished. Soon everyone began to understand that it was dangerous to oppose Hitler's government. They realised that they had lost their democratic right to a say in how their country was governed.

Dietrich had for some time been worried that Hitler would become too powerful. Very early on he had warned people in a radio broadcast: "The leader who makes an idol of himself and his office makes a mockery of God . . . God shall rule over you and you shall have no other Lord."

Next came an order excluding Jews from the Civil Service. In Hitler's view, Jews (not only people practising the Jewish religion, but anyone with Jewish or partly Jewish ancestry, however remote) were not Germans. Jews had their property and their jobs taken from them and many were thrown into prison and brutally treated. Dietrich, who had many Jewish friends and whose twin sister had married a Jew, was deeply concerned.

Things became worse. No one knew whether his neighbour was a friend or an enemy, for spies and informers were everywhere. Hitler proclaimed himself both Chancellor and President of Germany in July 1934 and anyone who stood in his way was imprisoned or murdered. He now planned to bring the rest of Europe under German domination. As a further step to this end he took Germany out of the League of Nations. (The League of Nations was established by a peace treaty after the First World War to try to prevent further wars. Britain, France, Italy and Japan were the founder members; Germany joined in 1926. The United Nations organisation later replaced the League of Nations.) Germany had for some time been steadily rearming for war.

The Church's struggle

The strong feeling of national unity had led to a movement to bring together all the separate Churches in Germany, to form a single Church. This new Church became known as the National Church. Troubled and divided almost from the start, it soon began to fall under government control.

Hitler demanded oaths of loyalty to himself from those in the Church. He wanted to use Christianity as a source of power to support his policies. Many of the people were already making Hitler their idol and were prepared to obey him without question, and there was a danger that the National Church would have to acknowledge Hitler, rather than Jesus Christ, as its overall leader.

Led by men such as Martin Neimöller, Dietrich and others threw themselves into the work of opposing Hitler's plans to place the Church under State control. They made a promise to preach solely from the Word of God, however dangerous this might prove to be.

Dietrich did not think that German churchmen were taking a firm enough stand against Hitler. He warned them that they were drifting away from true Christianity, and that the future of the Church was in grave danger. This made him unpopular. Even some of his friends were critical of him. Discouraged, he felt he should go away for a while and do pastoral work, simply and humbly. In October 1933 he started work as a pastor to a German Protestant community in London.

While he was in London Dietrich kept in close touch with Germany. He often spoke with Bishop Bell and together they watched anxiously as Hitler tried to make the Church give him its approval, so that the people would believe that what he was doing was right. When he did not get what he wanted, Hitler began to undermine the Church.

In January 1934 came an announcement that all pastors in Germany were forbidden to criticise the government in public. This made it very hard for them to preach with honesty. Some, fearing for their lives, preached patriotism and praised Hitler. Others, no longer able to accept Hitler's demands, made an open declaration of faith. Their declaration read: "Jesus Christ, as He is testified to us in Holy Scripture, is the one Word of God which we have to hear, and which we have to trust and obey in life and death." They promised to "deliver to all men, by means of preaching and sacrament, the message of the Free Grace of God". With this statement, the Confessing Church of Germany was officially born.

It was time for Dietrich to return to Germany. By the time he left England in the spring of 1935, with the help of Bishop Bell he had gained strong support for the German Church leaders who were resisting Nazi oppression.

Finkenwalde

Dietrich was appointed director of a preachers' seminary (training college) which the Confessing Church had illegally founded. He believed that a new Church must arise, based on obedience to God's Word. Its growth would depend on a group of dedicated young men living according to Jesus's teachings in the Sermon on the Mount.

Dietrich gathered together his first twenty-five students and searched for a suitable place for the seminary. The first few weeks were spent on the shores of the Baltic Sea in a ramshackle conference centre. Soon afterwards a more permanent home was found in a rambling country house outside the small village of Finkenwalde, east of Stettin (now called Szczecin). The house was empty and half derelict, but the students set to work at once. They had very little money, but they scrubbed and painted the rooms, dug the garden and planted vegetables. They went on begging expeditions in the neighbourhood, coming back with gifts of food and furniture. Dietrich brought all his books from Berlin for them to use.

Unexpected help came from Ruth von Kleist, a fine old lady who lived in Stettin. Greatly troubled by what was happening in Germany, she loved the Confessing Church and was willing to do anything she could to protect it. She also believed that her wealth belonged to God, and when the seminary's food stores were low a cartload of meat and vegetables would appear at Finkenwalde.

Dietrich's students knew what it meant to be in danger. Because they had refused to swear an oath of loyalty to Hitler or serve in the National Church (now an instrument of Nazi policy) they were breaking the law. They had come to Finkenwalde because they were ready to sacrifice themselves for the freedom to live and preach the truth as they saw it.

At Finkenwalde, the day began with prayer, singing and lessons from the Bible. Breakfast followed. Then the students were to meditate for half an hour, in silence, on a passage of Scripture. The young men found this difficult. What, they asked, were they to do in this silent half hour? Could they smoke, or get on with their reading? Dietrich said no, and explained how the heart and mind must learn to listen. His own stillness and concentration helped to teach them the value of quiet, intense prayer.

When they left Finkenwalde, the students had little hope of getting a normal pastor's job. Hardly a day passed when members or former members of the Confessing Church were not imprisoned. Dietrich wrote to all his former students and tried to encourage them to stand firm. They were under constant pressure to swear loyalty to Hitler and thus avoid persecution by the Nazis.

For a long time the seminary escaped the notice of the authorities, but the risk of discovery grew daily. Dietrich asked his students whether any of them would like to leave. Not one did. They accepted cheerfully the risk of being outlaws and the work of Finkenwalde continued under increasing secrecy. Inspired by his pupils' courage, Dietrich was writing an important work called *The Cost of Discipleship*.

The last course at the seminary ended on 8 September 1936. Twenty days later Finkenwalde was discovered and closed down. Dietrich spent the next two years in remote provinces of Pomerania, secretly training small groups of young pastors.

What was his Christian duty?

During the next few years, the persecution of the Jews became more and more horrific. Jewish homes, shops and synagogues were burnt down; Jews were denied German citizenship and forbidden to travel. It was becoming very clear that Hitler was power-crazy and that he would stop at nothing to achieve his dream: Germany as conqueror of Europe, with himself as supreme dictator.

In 1939 men of Dietrich's age were due to be called up for military service. On Christian grounds, Dietrich was against war, but he would have fought for his country if he had believed the cause was just. He could not fight for a Nazi State, however, and he would not serve a government that was leading its people into war. The problem was that his refusal to go into the army might bring the Confessing Church further under suspicion. It seemed to Dietrich that, much though he loved his country, he could best serve it now by leaving it. In the spring of 1939 he left for England.

In England, he was asked to take on a chaplaincy for refugees in New York. Not at all sure that he had made the correct decision, in June 1939 he set sail for America.

Soon afterwards he wrote: "It is now quite clear to me again that I must return to my work." He felt that training pastors for the Confessing Church was more important than ever now that the National Church was under Nazi domination. The truth of God's Word had to be preached.

Dietrich had been able to follow an honourable course up to now, fighting for the freedom to teach and preach. Now he was going back to be totally involved with the Resistance, plotting the downfall of the Nazis, regardless of the consequences. He would be forced to forsake many of the demands of Christian life when he became a political enemy of Hitler, and this worried him. He might have to condone violence, which he had always opposed. He was convinced that this was the only way to defend all he believed in, but it was a bitter decision.

Before he sailed for Germany, he wrote to a friend: "I will have no right to help with the rebuilding of Christian life in Germany after the war if I do not share the trials of this time with my people."

War

On 14 March 1939 Hitler's armies marched into Czechoslovakia. Encouraged by the lack of resistance, they attacked Poland in September, and occupied Warsaw. News arrived that special troops, acting on Hitler's orders, had behaved with horrible cruelty towards the Polish people. Alarmed, Britain gave Hitler forty-eight hours to withdraw his troops. He ignored the ultimatum. Britain, and then France, declared war on Germany.

Hitler invaded and occupied Norway, Belgium and Holland. It seemed as though nothing could stop him. His armies pressed on into France and in June 1940 the French surrendered. Hitler's successes convinced many Germans that he was a great leader and his popularity increased. The Resistance realised they were in for a long struggle.

Hitler now prepared to invade the last stronghold in Europe: Britain. But when he sent his aircraft across the Channel to bomb Britain, they were defeated by the R.A.F.

Rouen falls to the Germans as they sweep through France, 1940

in small fighter planes. The Battle of Britain was Hitler's first setback. The tide was beginning to turn against him.

Most historians agree that the 'Tide' turned against Nazi Germany at the end of Jan 1943. With the surrender of the 6th Army after the Battle of Stalingrad. The Wehrmacht lost over 100,000 men - the survivors went into captivity - many never returned

Resistance

On his return to Germany, Dietrich began to work secretly for the Resistance under cover of his work for the Confessing Church. He was also recruited by the goverment's Counter Espionage Department, which meant that he was acting as a sort of double agent. His work for the goverment allowed him some freedom to move about and helped him with his Resistance work.

Quite soon, however, he was accused of "subversive activity" when the police found him talking to a group of students after a lecture in a conference centre. Any public meeting was illegal and Dietrich now had to report regularly to the police. This meant that he could no longer be of much use to his Church.

The mass murder of Jews in concentration camps had begun. Whenever he could, Dietrich helped small groups of Jews to escape over the border into Switzerland. As he suspected, he was being watched by the secret police, and soon another blow fell. He was forbidden to publish any of his written work.

During this time he and his friends often had grave conversations about the duty of a Christian. He was asked the meaning of a passage in the Bible where Jesus warns His disciples, "They that take the sword shall perish by the sword." Dietrich replied that it meant exactly what it said. All Christians must accept the fact that they, too, came under Divine judgement, even when they felt they must commit acts of violence to achieve something they believed was right.

In the winter of 1941/2 Dietrich said he was willing to be involved in a plot on Hitler's life if necessary (various unsuccessful assassination attempts had already been made). He would need a little warning, though, to give him time to resign from the Confessing Church. He knew his Church would not approve of any act of violence.

When a fellow prisoner later asked him how, as a Christian, he could take part in active resistance against Hitler, Dietrich answered: "If I saw a drunken driver racing down the street, I would not consider it my duty to bury the victims of the madman. It would be more important to wrench the wheel out of his hands."

In May 1942 Dietrich was sent by the Resistance to meet Bishop Bell in Stockholm. The Resistance wanted to know whether Britain would hold peace talks with a new German government if Hitler was overthrown. Dietrich assured the Bishop that Germany would expect to pay for her war deeds. The Bishop returned to England and did all he could to persuade the British government to agree to discuss peace plans, but it was no use. Britain would accept nothing less than Germany's total surrender.

His engagement

Dietrich went to spend a few weeks with his old friend Ruth von Kleist, who now lived outside Berlin. Here he met her granddaughter, Maria von Wedemeyer, whom he had last seen when she was a child. Now she was a beautiful young woman and Dietrich fell in love with her. He could not believe she might feel the same way about him; she was seventeen years younger than him. They met often in Berlin, however, and to his joy he found that Maria loved him too.

Maria's father had been killed and now news came of her brother's death at the front. Her mother, unable to bear the thought of losing Maria, asked Dietrich to agree to a year's

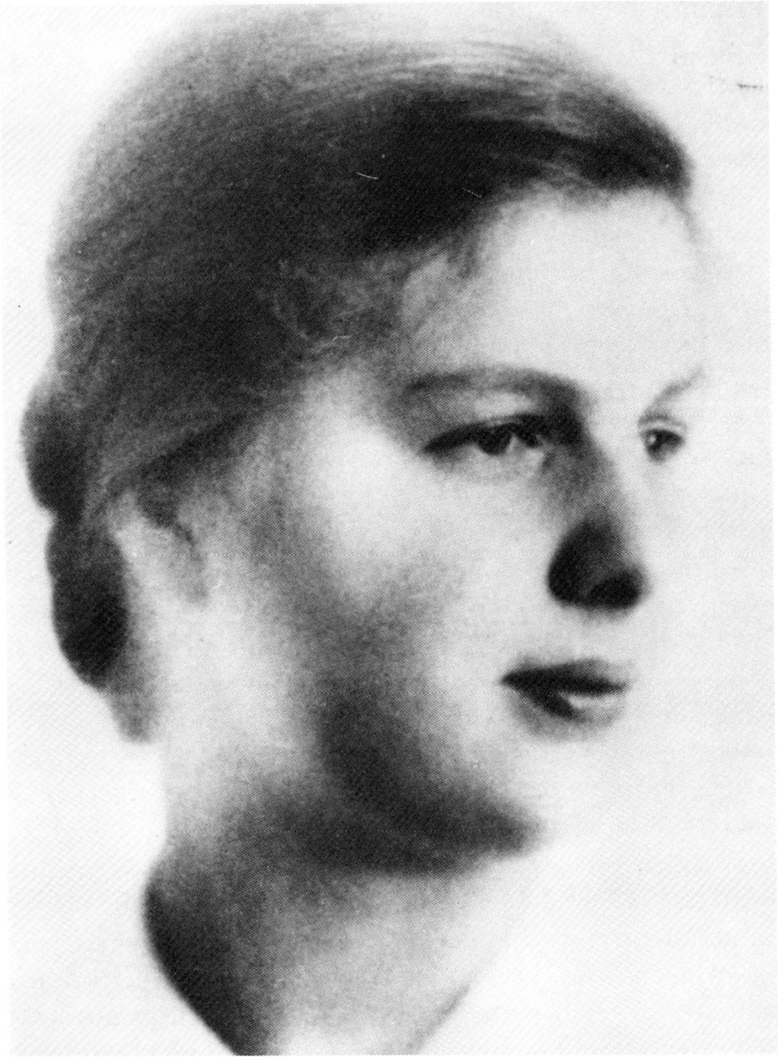

Maria von Wedemeyer

separation from her. Reluctantly he agreed, but in the end Maria's mother gave way to her pleas and on 17 January 1943 Dietrich and Maria became engaged.

Arrest

During the winter of 1942/3 plans for the assassination of Hitler were completed. Dietrich was involved in the plot. But once again Hitler escaped. The bomb failed to go off and all attempts to overthrow the government had to be abandoned.

Meanwhile the net was closing on the leaders of the Resistance. Dietrich was under suspicion because he had helped Jews to escape and because he had avoided military service. His part in the assassination plot was not discovered until later but there was enough evidence to convict him. On 5 April 1943 the secret police came to the Bonhoeffers' house and arrested him. Without any explanation they asked him to come with them and drove him to Tegel Military Prison.

The iron gates clanged behind him and he was locked in a cell. Each day Dietrich continued the discipline of his Christian life, reading the Bible, meditating, and praising God. His letters home did not mention the hardships he suffered. He made friends with some of the warders as well as his fellow prisoners. One of them said afterwards, "His soul really shone in the darkness of prison life."

Other Resistance leaders had been arrested at the same time as Dietrich, some of them close friends of his. Now the core of the Resistance was threatened, and it was important that the prisoners should stick to pre-arranged answers under questioning so that they would not endanger the lives of their friends. They kept in touch with the Resistance through secret messages carried for them by their visitors.

Dietrich was visited by his parents and Maria and the warders sometimes allowed him a few minutes in private with them if it was safe. These were the brighter moments that gave him hope, but as time passed he was thrown from one dark mood to another. There were many hours when there was nothing to do but think. He longed for Maria. He

Dietrich with four Italian prisoners and a German officer in the yard of Tegel Prison, 1944

had now spent over a year in prison, and only his strong self-discipline kept him sane. He read a great deal and was writing a series of religious letters.

As the Allies advanced towards Germany the air raids increased. Dietrich always remained perfectly calm through the raids, comforting the guards and the prisoners. He was able to help the wounded because he knew something about first aid.

Finally the time came when he was allowed no more visitors. Even Maria was turned away. The war was drawing to a close and Berlin was being heavily bombed.

One day the prisoners were ordered to assemble in the prison yard. Dietrich was taken in a truck with other prisoners to a prison at Flossenbürg, where he met up with some old friends. It was almost a happy time as they renewed old memories and talked about the future, when Germany would be free from Nazi rule.

Seven weeks passed. Then, on Easter Sunday, the guns of

Flossenbürg

the Allies were heard. The prisoners hoped this meant they would soon be freed. That night two guards rounded up the prisoners for a "trial". They were all condemned to die. Early the next morning, between five and six o'clock, the verdicts were read out to them. Then they were ordered to strip.

Naked, and for the last time, Dietrich knelt to pray. A few minutes later he was hanged. It was 9 April 1945 and Dietrich was thirty-nine years old. Below his memorial in the church at Flossenbürg are the words: "Dietrich Bonhoeffer – a Witness of Jesus Christ among his brethren".

Three weeks later Hitler committed suicide. Germany surrendered and the surviving victims of the Nazis were released.

BIOGRAPHICAL NOTES

4 February 1906 Dietrich Bonhoeffer is born in Breslau, Germany.

1923 Dietrich goes to Tübingen University to study theology.

1924 Continues his studies at Berlin University.

1928 Works as assistant pastor in Barcelona.

September 1930 Leaves to spend a year at the Union Theological Seminary in New York.

1931 Ordained.

August 1931 Appointed lecturer at Berlin University.

January 1933 Hitler becomes Chancellor of Germany.

April 1933 Boycott of Jewish businesses in Germany.

October 1933 Dietrich becomes pastor to a Lutheran congregation in London.

1934 Confessing Church of Germany comes into being.

Spring 1935 Dietrich is appointed director of preachers' seminary, which settles at Finkenwalde.

October 1936 Finkenwalde closes. Dietrich continues working for the Confessing Church.

November 1937 *The Cost of Discipleship* published.

9 November 1938 "Crystal Night". Jewish synagogues and shops burnt to the ground.

March 1939 Hitler invades Czechoslovakia.

June 1939 Dietrich sets sail for America to undertake a chaplaincy for refugees in New York.

July 1939 Returns to Germany and takes charge of a preachers' seminary in Sigurdshof.

September 1939 Invasion of Poland. Britain declares war.

March 1940 Sigurdshof closed. Dietrich becomes increasingly involved with the Resistance.

May 1942 Meeting with Bishop Bell in Stockholm.

January 1943 Engagement to Maria von Wedemeyer.

5 April 1943 Arrested and taken to Tegel prison.

9 April 1945 Hanged in Flossenbürg concentration camp.

Maria von Wedemeyer

THINGS TO DO

A Test yourself

Here are some short questions. See if you can remember the answers from what you have read. Then write them down in a few words.

1. What was the most important thing Dietrich learnt from his parents?
2. Where did the Bonhoeffer family spend the summer holidays?
3. What was the fault in his character that Dietrich struggled to overcome?
4. What impressed Dietrich about church services in Harlem?
5. Why did the German people vote for Hitler's Nazi Party?
6. In his sermon to the confirmation class, what did Dietrich say he wanted the boys to have?
7. What did Dietrich do when he returned to Germany in the spring of 1935, after working in London?
8. In which year did Germany invade Czechoslovakia and Poland?
9. Why was Dietrich forced to report regularly to the police?
10. Give one reason why Dietrich was under suspicion in 1943.

B Think through

These questions need longer answers. Think about them, and then try to write two or three sentences in answer to each one. You may look up the story again to help you.

1. What did Dietrich think of the students he met in America?
2. Describe conditions in Germany in 1931.
3. In what ways did Hitler restrict personal freedom?
4. What was Hitler's attitude to the Church?
5. Why did Dietrich leave Germany in the spring of 1939?
6. Dietrich found it hard to make the decision to work for the Resistance. Why?
7. What was the purpose of Dietrich's meeting with Bishop Bell in Stockholm?

C To talk about

Here are some questions for you to discuss together. Try to give reasons for what you say or think. Try to find out all the different opinions which people have about each question.

1 Do you think we should try to recognise and overcome our faults, or is it impossible for anyone to change their character?
2 There are many different denominations in the Christian Church. Would it be better if they were all united as one Church?
3 Could German pastors have preached with honesty from the Bible if they obeyed Hitler?
4 Jesus said, "Happy are you when people insult you and persecute you because you are My followers." What does this mean? Do you think it takes courage to admit you are a Christian today? Think about people who have suffered for their faith: Richard Wurmbrand, for example (see page 29).
5 Is it ever right to break the law (peacefully or with violence) in order to uphold an idea or a religious belief? You could discuss people like Brother Andrew (see page 29) and think about the methods used by members of the peace movement in their campaign for nuclear disarmament, for example.
6 Do you think Dietrich was right to involve himself in a plot to kill Hitler?

D Find out

Choose one or two of the subjects below and find out all you can about them. History books, geography books and encyclopaedias may be useful. Perhaps you can use reference books in your school or public library to look up some of the names and places.

1 *Germany*
   (a) Draw a map of Europe and colour in all the countries occupied by Germany in the Second World War.
   (b) How was Germany divided up at the end of the war? What marks the boundary between East and West Germany?

(c) Draw a map showing Berlin, Munich, the Harz Mountains, Szczecin, Tübingen and Wroclaw. Which of these places are no longer in Germany?

2 *The Church*

(a) Read about the life of Martin Luther. Why did his beliefs lead to a division of the Church? In which countries are there large numbers of Lutherans today?

(b) Write a short account of the Reformation in Britain.

(c) Which gospels tell the story of the Sermon on the Mount? For whom do you think Jesus's message was principally intended?

3 *The Jews*

(a) What happened in Germany on "Crystal Night"?

(b) Draw a map of Europe and mark on it all the places where there were concentration camps for Jews. How many Jews were killed in these camps?

(c) When was the new State of Israel founded? Write a brief account of its early history.

(d) Find out about other people who helped Jews during the Second World War, such as Corrie ten Boom (see page 29) and Raul Wallenberg.

USEFUL INFORMATION

More books to read

Bible Smuggler: Brother Andrew, by David Wallington (R.M.E.P.) (P).

The Secret Room: Corrie ten Boom, by David Wallington (R.M.E.P.) (P).

Trial of Faith: Richard Wurmbrand, by R.J. Owen (R.M.E.P.) (P).

Books by Dietrich Bonhoeffer (translated from the German):
Christology (Fontana) (T).
The Cost of Discipleship (S.C.M. Press) (T).
Ethics (Fontana) (T).
Life Together (S.C.M. Press) (T).
Prayers from Prison (Collins) (T).

Books about Dietrich Bonhoeffer:

Bonhoeffer, an Illustrated Introduction, by Eberhard Bethge (Collins) (T).

Bonhoeffer, True Patriot, by Mary Bosanquet (Mowbray) (T).

Dietrich Bonhoeffer, edited by E.J. Tinsley (Epworth) (T).

In Pursuit of Dietrich Bonhoeffer, by William Kuhns (Burns & Oates; Anthony Clarke Books) (T).

The Life and Death of Dietrich Bonhoeffer, by Mary Bosanquet (Hodder & Stoughton) (T).

DIETRICH BONHOEFFER · MARY BOSANQUET and EBERHARD BETHGE

(T) = suitable for teachers and older pupils
(P) = suitable for younger pupils

BON.HOEFFER - STEPHEN PLANT

Film

A Life of Challenge (28 min), colour. Short film portrait of Dietrich Bonhoeffer, drawing on the recollections of his family and friends. Available from Concord Films Council, 201 Felixstowe Road, Ipswich IP3 9BJ.

Play

The Conspirator, by Don Shaw. Play based on Eberhard Bethge's *Bonhoeffer, an Illustrated Introduction* (see above). Copies of the script can be bought from Derby Playhouse, Theatre Walk, Eagle Centre, Derby DE1 2NF. For adults.

These extracts are taken from a chapter entitled "German Moralities"
in "The 3rd Reich at War" - by Richard J. EVANS

In 1939 the overwhelming majority of Germans still steered
their moral life mainly by the compass of the Christian religion
When WW2 started 95% of Germans described themselves
Either as Catholics or as Protestants, 3.5% were "Deists"
and 1.5% atheists: most people in these latter categories
were convinced Nazis who had left their Church at the
behest of the Party, which had been been trying since the
mid-30's to reduce the influence of Christianity in society
The Catholic Church had most adherents in the South
and west of Germany; The Protestants were prominent in North and
Central Germany. Hitler hostility to Christianity reached new
heights, or depths during WW2. After the war was over and
victory assured he said in 1942, the Concordat he had signed
with the Catholic Church in 1933 would be formally abrogated
and the Church would be dealt with like any other non-Nazi
voluntary association. The 3rd Reich would not tolerate
the intervention of any foreign influences such as the Pope.
Priests he said were "black bugs", abortions in cassocks.
Hitler emphasised again and again his belief that Nazism
was a secular ideology founded on modern science. Science
he declared would destroy the last vestiges of superstitions
"The best thing" he declared on Oct 14 1941, "is to let Christianity
die a natural death. A slow death has something
comforting about it. It was indelibly Jewish in origin and
character." "Christianity is a prototype of Bolshevism